D1736552

Astrophel and Stella

Philip Sidney

Table of Contents

Astrophel and Stella

Philip Sidney

I

Ouing in trueth, and fayne in verse my loue to show,
That she, deare Shee, might take som pleasure of my paine,
Pleasure might cause her reade, reading might make her know,
Knowledge might pittie winne, and pity grace obtaine,
I sought fit wordes to paint the blackest face of woe;
Studying inuentions fine, her wits to entertaine,
Oft turning others leaues, to see if thence would flow
Some fresh and fruitfull showers vpon my sun–burnd brain.
But words came halting forth, wanting Inuentions stay;
Inuention, Natures childe, fledde step–dame Studies blowes;
And others feet still seemde but strangers in my way.
Thus, great with childe to speak, and helplesse in my throwes,
Biting my trewand pen, beating myselfe for spite,
Fool, said my Muse to me, looke in thy heart, and write.

II

Not at the first sight, nor with a dribbed shot,
Loue gaue the wound, which, while I breathe, will bleede;
But knowne worth did in tract of time proceed,
Till by degrees, it had full conquest got.
I saw and lik'd; I lik'd but loued not;

I lou'd, but straight did not what Loue decreed:
At length, to Loues decrees I, forc'd, agreed,
Yet with repining at so partiall lot.
Now, euen that footstep of lost libertie
Is gone; and now, like slaue–borne Muscouite,
I call it praise to suffer tyrannie;
And nowe imploy the remnant of my wit
To make myselfe beleeue that all is well,
While, with a feeling skill, I paint my hell.

III

Let dainty wits crie on the Sisters nine,
That, brauely maskt, their fancies may be told;
Or, Pindars apes, flaunt they in phrases fine,
Enam'ling with pied flowers their thoughts of gold;
Or else let them in statlier glorie shine,
Ennobling new–found tropes with problemes old;
Or with strange similes enrich each line,
Of herbes or beasts which Inde or Affrick hold.
For me, in sooth, no Muse but one I know,
Phrases and problems from my reach do grow;
And strange things cost too deare for my poor sprites.
How then? euen thus: in Stellaes face I reed
What Loue and Beautie be; then all my deed
But copying is, what in her Nature writes.

IV

Vertue, alas, now let me take some rest;
Thou setst a bate betweene my will and wit;
If vaine Loue haue my simple soule opprest,
Leaue what thou lik'st not, deale thou not with it.
Thy scepter vse in some old Catoes brest,

Churches or Schooles are for thy seat more fit;
I do confesse (pardon a fault confest)
My mouth too tender is for thy hard bit.
But if that needes thou wilt vsurping be
The little reason that is left in me,
And still th'effect of thy perswasions prooue,
I sweare, my heart such one shall show to thee,
That shrines in flesh so true a deitie,
That, Virtue, thou thyself shalt be in loue.

V

It is most true that eyes are form'd to serue
The inward light, and that the heauenly part
Ought to be King, from whose rules who do swerue,
Rebels to nature, striue for their owne smart.
It is most true, what we call Cupids dart
An image is, which for ourselues we carue,
And, foolse, adore in temple of our hart,
Till that good god make church and churchmen starue.
True, that true beautie virtue is indeed,
Whereof this beautie can be but a shade,
Which, elements with mortal mixture breed.
True, that on earth we are but pilgrims made,
And should in soule up to our countrey moue:
True, and yet true that I must Stella loue.

VI

Some louers speake, when they their Muses entertaine,
Of hopes begot by feare, of wot not what desires,
Of force of heau'nly beames infusing hellish paine,
Of liuing deaths, dere wounds, faire storms, and freesing fires:
Some one his song in Ioue and Ioues strange tales attires,

3

Bordred with buls and swans, powdred with golden raine:
Another, humbler wit, to shepherds pipe retires,
Yet hiding royall bloud full oft in rurall vaine.
To some a sweetest plaint a sweetest stile affords:
While teares poure out his inke, and sighes breathe out his words,
His paper pale despaire, and pain his pen doth moue.
I can speake what I feele, and feele as much as they,
But thinke that all the map of my state I display
When trembling voyce brings forth, that I do Stella loue.

VII

When Nature made her chief worke, Stellas eyes,
In colour blacke why wrapt she beames so bright?
Would she in beamy blacke, like Painter wise,
Frame daintiest lustre, mixt of shades and light?
Or did she else that sober hue deuise,
In obiect best to knitt and strength our sight;
Least, if no vaile these braue gleames did disguise,
They, sunlike, should more dazle then delight?
Or would she her miraculous power show,
That, whereas blacke seems Beauties contrary,
She euen in black doth make all beauties flow?
Both so, and thus, she, minding Loue should be
Plac'd euer there, gaue him this mourning weede
To honour all their deaths who for her bleed.

VIII

Loue, borne in Greece, of late fled from his natiue place,
Forc't, by a tedious proof, that Turkish hardned heart
Is not fit mark to pierce with his fine–pointed dart,
And pleas'd with our soft peace, staide here his flying race:
But, finding these north clymes too coldly him embrace,

Not vsde to frozen clips, he straue to find some part
Where with most ease and warmth he might employ his art;
At length he perch'd himself in Stellaes ioyful face,
Whose faire skin, beamy eyes, like morning sun on snow,
Deceiu'd the quaking boy, who thought, from so pure light,
Effects of liuely heat must needs in nature grow:
But she, most faire, most cold, made him thence take his flight
To my close heart, where, while some firebrands he did lay,
He burnt vn'wares his wings, and cannot flie away.

IX

Queen Virtues Court, which some call Stellaes face,
Prepar'd by Natures choicest furniture,
Hath his front built of alabaster pure;
Gold is the couering of that stately place.
The door, by which sometimes comes forth her grace,
Red porphir is, which locke of pearl makes sure,
Whose porches rich (which name of chekes indure)
Marble, mixt red and white, doe interlace.
The windowes now, through which this heau'nly guest
Looks ouer the world, and can find nothing such,
Which dare claime from those lights the name of best,
Of touch they are, that without touch do touch,
Which Cupids self, from Beauties mine did draw:
Of touch they are, and poore I am their straw.

X

Reason, in faith thou art well seru'd that still
Wouldst brabbling be with Sense and Loue in me;
I rather wisht thee clime the Muses hill;
Or reach the fruite of Natures choycest tree;
Or seek heau'ns course or heau'ns inside to see:

Why shouldst thou toil our thorny soile to till?
Leaue Sense, and those which Senses obiects be;
Deale thou with powers of thoughts, leaue Loue to Will.
But thou wouldst needs fight with both Loue and Sence,
With sword of wit giuing wounds of dispraise,
Till downe–right blowes did foyle thy cunning fence;
For, soone as they strake thee with Stellas rayes,
Reason, thou kneeld'st, and offred'st straight to proue,
By reason good, good reason her to loue.

XI

In truth, O Loue, with what a boyish kind
Thou doest proceed in thy most serious ways,
That when the heau'n to thee his best displayes,
Yet of that best thou leau'st the best behinde!
For, like a childe that some faire booke doth find,
With gilded leaues or colour'd vellum playes,
Or, at the most, on some fine picture stayes,
But neuer heeds the fruit of Writers mind;
So when thou saw'st, in Natures cabinet,
Stella, thou straight lookst babies in her eyes:
In her chekes pit thou didst thy pitfold set,
And in her breast bo–peepe or crouching lies,
Playing and shining in each outward part;
But, fool, seekst not to get into her heart.

XII

Cupid, because thou shin'st in Stellaes eyes
That from her locks thy day–nets none scapes free
That those lips sweld so full of thee they be
That her sweet breath makes oft thy flames to rise
That in her breast thy pap well sugred lies

That her grace gracious makes thy wrongsthat she,
What words soere shee speake, perswades for thee
That her clere voice lifts thy fame to the skies,
Thou countest Stella thine, like those whose pow'rs
Hauing got vp a breach by fighting well,
Crie Victorie, this faire day all is ours!
O no; her heart is such a cittadell,
So fortified with wit, stor'd with disdaine,
That to win it is all the skill and paine.

XIII

Phoebus was iudge betweene Ioue, Mars, and Loue,
Of those three gods, whose armes the fairest were.
Ioues golden shield did sable eagles beare,
Whose talons held young Ganimed aboue:
But in vert field Mars bare a golden speare,
Which through a bleeding heart his point did shoue:
Each had his creast; Mars carried Venus gloue,
Ioue on his helmet the thunderbolt did reare.
Cupid then smiles, for on his crest there lies
Stellas faire haire; her face he makes his shield,
Where roses gules are borne in siluer field.
Phoebus drew wide the curtaines of the skies,
To blaze these last, and sware deuoutly then,
The first, thus matcht, were scantly gentlemen.

XIV

Alas, haue I not pain enough, my friend,
Vpon whose breast a fiecer Gripe doth tire
Than did on him who first stale down the fire,
While Loue on me doth all his quiuer spend,
But with your rhubarbe words ye must contend

To grieue me worse, in saying that Desire
Doth plunge my wel–form'd soul euen in the mire
Of sinfull thoughts, which do in ruin end?
If that be sinne which doth the manners frame,
Well staid with truth in word and faith of deede,
Ready of wit, and fearing nought but shame;
If that be sin which in fixt hearts doth breed
A loathing of all loose vnchastitie,
Then loue is sin, and let me sinfull be.

XV

You that do search for euery purling spring
Which from the ribs of old Parnassus flowes,
And euery flower, not sweet perhaps, which growes
Neere thereabouts, into your poesie wring;
Ye that do dictionaries methode bring
Into your rimes, running in rattling rowes;
You that poore Petrarchs long deceased woes
With new–borne sighes and denisen'd wit do sing;
You take wrong wayes; those far–fet helps be such
As do bewray a want of inward tuch,
And sure, at length stol'n goods doe come to light:
But if, both for your loue and skill, your name
You seek to nurse at fullest breasts of Fame,
Stella behold, and then begin to indite.

XVI

In nature, apt to like, when I did see
Beauties which were of many carrets fine,
My boiling sprites did thither then incline,
And, Loue, I thought that I was full of thee:
But finding not those restlesse flames in mee,

Which others said did make their souls to pine,
I thought those babes of some pinnes hurt did whine,
By my soul iudging what Loues paine might be.
But while I thus with this young lion plaid,
Mine eyes (shall I say curst or blest?) beheld
Stella: now she is nam'd, neede more be said?
In her sight I a lesson new haue speld.
I now haue learnd loue right, and learnd euen so
As they that being poysond poyson know.

XVII

His mother deere, Cupid offended late,
Because that Mars, growne slacker in her loue,
With pricking shot he did not throughly moue
To keepe the place of their first louing state.
The boy refusde for fear of Marses hate,
Who threatned stripes if he his wrath did proue;
But she, in chafe, him from her lap did shoue,
Brake bowe, brake shafts, while Cupid weeping sate;
Till that his grandame Nature, pitying it,
Of Stellaes brows made him two better bowes,
And in her eyes of arrows infinit.
O how for ioy he leaps! O how he crowes!
And straight therewith, like wags new got to play,
Falls to shrewd turnes! And I was in his way.

XVIII

With what sharp checkes I in myself am shent
When into Reasons audite I do goe,
And by iust counts my selfe a bankrout know
Of all those goods which heauen to me hath lent;
Vnable quite to pay euen Natures rent,

Which vnto it by birthright I do ow;
And, which is worse, no good excuse can showe,
But that my wealth I haue most idly spent!
My youth doth waste, my knowledge brings forth toyes,
My wit doth striue those passions to defende,
Which, for reward, spoil it with vain annoyes.
I see, my course to lose myself doth bend;
I see: and yet no greater sorrow take
Than that I lose no more for Stellas sake.

XIX

On Cupids bowe how are my heart–strings bent,
That see my wracke, and yet embrace the same!
When most I glory, then I feele most shame;
I willing run, yet while I run repent;
My best wits still their own disgrace inuent:
My very inke turns straight to Stellas name;
And yet my words, as them my pen doth frame,
Auise them selues that they are vainely spent:
For though she passe all things, yet what is all
That vnto me, who fare like him that both
Lookes to the skies and in a ditch doth fall?
O let me prop my mind, yet in his growth,
And not in nature for best fruits vnfit.
Scholler, saith Loue, bend hitherward your wit.

XX

Fly, fly, my friends; I haue my deaths wound, fly;
See there that Boy, that murthring Boy I say,
Who like a theefe hid in dark bush doth ly,
Till bloudy bullet get him wrongfull pray.
So, tyran he no fitter place could spie,

Nor so faire leuell in so secret stay,
As that sweet black which veils the heau'nly eye;
There with his shot himself he close doth lay.
Poore passenger, pass now thereby I did,
And staid, pleas'd with the prospect of the place,
While that black hue from me the the bad guest hid:
But straight I saw the motions of lightning grace,
And then descried the glistrings of his dart:
But ere I could flie thence, it pierc'd my heart.

XXI

Your words, my friend, (right healthfull caustiks), blame
My young mind marde, whom Loue doth windlas so;
That mine owne writings, like bad seruants, show
My wits quicke in vaine thoughts, in vertue lame;
That Plato I read for nought but if he tame
Such coltish yeeres; that to my birth I owe
Nobler desires, lest else that friendly foe,
Great expectation, wear a train of shame:
For since mad March great promise made of mee,
If now the May of my yeeres much decline,
What can be hop'd my haruest–time will be?
Sure, you say well, Your wisedomes golden myne
Dig deepe with Learnings spade. Now tell me this:
Hath this world aught so fair as Stella is?

XXII

In highest way of heau'n the Sun did ride,
Progressing then from fair Twinnes golden place,
Hauing no mask of clouds before his face,
But streaming forth of heate in his chiefe pride;
When some fair ladies, by hard promise tied,

On horsebacke met him in his furious race;
Yet each prepar'd with fannes wel—shading grace
From that foes wounds their tender skinnes to hide.
Stella alone with face vnarmèd marcht,
Either to do like him which open shone,
Or carelesse of the wealth, because her owne.
Yet were the hid and meaner beauties parcht;
Her dainties bare went free: the cause was this:
The sun, that others burn'd, did her but kisse.

XXIII

The curious wits, seeing dull pensiuenesse
Bewray it self in my long—settl'd eies
Whence those same fumes of melancholy rise,
With idle paines and missing ayme do guesse.
Some, that know how my spring I did addresse,
Deem that my Muse some fruit of knowledge plies;
Others, because the prince my seruice tries,
Thinke that I think State errours to redress:
But harder iudges iudge ambitions rage:
Scourge of itselfe, still climbing slipperie place:
Holds my young brain captiu'd in golden cage.
O fooles, or ouer—wise. alas, the race
Of all my thoughts hath neither stop nor start
But only Stellaes eyes and Stellaes heart.

XXIV

Rich fooles there be whose base and filthy heart
Lies hatching still the goods wherein they flow,
And damning their own selues to Tantals smart,
Wealth breeding want; more rich, more wretched growe:
Yet to those fooles Heau'n doth such wit impart

As what their hands do hold, their heads do know,
And knowing loue, and louing lay apart
As sacred things, far from all dangers show.
But that rich foole, who by blind Fortunes lot
The richest gemme of loue and life enioys,
And can with foule abuse such beauties blot;
Let him, depriu'd of sweet but vnfelt ioys,
Exild for ay from those high treasures which
He knowes not, grow in only folly rich!

XXV

The wisest scholler of the wight most wise
By Phoebus doom, with sugred sentence sayes,
That vertue, if it once met with our eyes,
Strange flames of loue it in our souls would raise;
But for that man with paine this truth descries,
Whiles he each thing in Senses balance wayes,
And so nor will nor can behold those skies
Which inward sunne to heroick mind displaies
Vertue of late, with vertuous care to ster
Loue of herself, tooke Stellas shape, that she
To mortall eyes might sweetly shine in her.
It is most true; for since I her did see,
Vertues great beauty in that face I proue,
And find th' effect, for I do burn in loue.

XXVI

Though dustie wits dare scorne Astrologie,
And fooles can thinke those lampes of purest light
Whose numbers, waies, greatnesse, eternity,
Promising wonders, wonder do inuite
To haue for no cause birthright in the sky

But for to spangle the black weeds of Night;
Or for some brawl which in that chamber hie,
They should still dance to please a gazers sight.
For me, I do Nature vnidle know,
And know great causes great effects procure;
And know those bodies high raigne on the low.
And if these rules did fail, proof makes me sure,
Who oft fore–see my after–following race,
By only those two starres in Stellaes face.

XXVII

Because I oft in darke abstracted guise
Seeme most alone in greatest company,
With dearth of words, or answers quite awrie,
To them that would make speech of speech arise;
They deeme, and of their doome the runour flies,
That poison foul of bubbling pride doth lie
So in my swelling breast, that only I
Fawne on my selfe, and others do despise.
Yet pride I thinke doth not my soule possesse
(Which looks too oft in his vnflatt'ring glasse):
But one worse fault, ambition, I confesse,
That makes me oft my best friends ouerpasse,
Vnseene, vnheard, while thought to highest place
Bends all his powers, euen vnto Stellaes grace.

XXVIII

You that with Allegories curious frame
Of others children changelings vse to make,
With me those pains, for Gods sake, do not take:
I list not dig so deep for brazen fame,
When I say Stella I do meane the same

14

Princesse of beauty for whose only sake
The raines of Loue I loue, though neuer slake,
And ioy therein, though nations count it shame.
I beg no subiect to vse eloquence,
Nor in hid wayes to guide philosophy:
Looke at my hands for no such quintessence;
But know that I in pure simplicitie
Breathe out the flames which burn within my heart,
Loue onely reading vnto me this arte.

XXIX

Like some weak lords neighbord by mighty kings,
To keep themselues and their chief cities free,
Do easily yeeld that all their coasts may be
Ready to store their campes of needfull things;
So Stellas heart, finding what power Loue brings
To keep it selfe in life and liberty,
Doth willing graunt that in the frontiers he
Vse all to helpe his other conquerings.
And thus her heart escapes; but thus her eyes
Serue him with shot, her lips his heralds are,
Her breasts his tents, legs his triumphall car,
Her flesh his food, her skin his armour braue.
And I, but for because my prospect lies
Vpon that coast, am given vp for slaue.

XXX

Whether the Turkish new moone minded be
To fill her hornes this yeere on Christian coast;
How Poles right king means without leaue of host
To warm with ill-made fire cold Muscouy;
If French can yet three parts in one agree:

What now the Dutch in their full diets boast;
How Holland hearts, now so good townes be lost,
Trust in the shade of pleasant Orange–tree;
How Vlster likes of that same golden bit
Wherewith my father once made it half tame;
If in the Scotch Court be no weltring yet;
These questions busy wits to me do frame:
I, cumbred with good manners, answer doe,
But know not how; for still I thinke of you.

XXXI

With how sad steps, O Moone, thou climbst the skies!
How silently, and with how wanne a face!
What, may it be that euen in heau'nly place
That busie archer his sharpe arrowes tries?
Sure, if that long–with–loue–acquainted eyes
Can iudge of loue, thou feel'st a louers case,
I reade it in thy lookes: thy languist grace,
To me that feele the like, thy state discries.
Then, eu'n of fellowship, O Moone, tell me,
Is constant loue deem'd there but want of wit?
Are beauties there as proud as here they be?
Do they aboue loue to be lou'd, and yet
Those louers scorn whom that loue doth possesse?
Do they call vertue there vngratefulnesse?

XXXII

Morpheus, the liuely sonne of deadly Sleepe,
Witnesse of life to them that liuing die,
A prophet oft, and oft an historie,
A poet eke, as humours fly or creepe;
Since thou in me so sure a pow'r dost keepe,

That neuer I with clos'd–vp sense do lie,
But by thy worke my Stella I descrie,
Teaching blind eyes both how to smile and weepe;
Vouchsafe, of all acquaintance, this to tell,
Whence hast thou ivory, rubies, pearl, and gold,
To shew her skin, lips, teeth, and head so well?
Foole! answers he; no Indes such treasures hold;
But from thy heart, while my sire charmeth thee,
Sweet Stellas image I do steal to mee.

XXXIII

I might (vnhappy word!) O me, I might,
And then I would not, or could not, see my blisse,
Till now wrapt in a most infernall night,
I find how heau'nly day, wretch! I did misse.
Hart, rend thyself, thou dost thyself but right;
No louely Paris made thy Hellen his;
No force, no fraud robd thee of thy delight,
Nor Fortune of thy fortune author is,
But to my selfe my selfe did giue the blow,
While too much wit, forsooth, so troubled me
That I respects for both our sakes must show:
And yet could not, by rysing morne fore–see
How fair a day was near: O punisht eyes,
That I had bene more foolish, or more wise!

XXXIV

Come, let me write. And to what end? To ease
A burthen'd heart. How can words ease, which are
The glasses of thy dayly–vexing care?
Oft cruel fights well pictur'd–forth do please.
Art not asham'd to publish thy disease?

Nay, that may breed my fame, it is so rare.
But will not wise men thinke thy words fond ware?
Then be they close, and so none shall displease.
What idler thing then speake and not be hard?
What harder thing then smart and not to speake?
Peace, foolish wit! with wit my wit is mard.
Thus write I, while I doubt to write, and wreake
My harmes in inks poor losse. Perhaps some find
Stellas great pow'rs, that so confuse my mind.

XXXV

What may words say, or what may words not say,
Where Truth itself must speake like Flatterie?
Within what bounds can one his liking stay,
Where Nature doth with infinite agree?
What Nestors counsell can my flames alay,
Since Reasons self doth blow the coale in me?
And, ah, what hope that Hope should once see day,
Where Cupid is sworn page to Chastity?
Honour is honour'd that thou dost possesse
Him as thy slaue, and now long−needy Fame
Doth euen grow rich, meaning my Stellaes name.
Wit learnes in thee perfection to expresse:
Not thou by praise, but praise in thee is raisde:
It is a praise to praise, when thou art praisde.

XXXVI

Stella, whence doth these new assaults arise,
A conquerd yeelding ransackt heart to winne,
Whereto long since, through my long−battred eyes,
Whole armies of thy beauties entred in?
And there, long since, Loue, thy lieutenant, lies;

18

My forces razde, thy banners raisd within:
Of conquest, do not these effects suffice,
But wilt new warre vpon thine own begin?
With so sweet voice, and by sweet Nature so
In sweetest stratagems sweete Art can show,
That not my soul, which at thy foot did fall
Long since, forc'd by thy beams, but stone nor tree,
By Sences priviledge, can scape from thee!

XXXVII

My mouth doth water, and my breast doth swell,
My tongue doth itch, my thoughts in labour be:
Listen then, lordings, with good ear to me,
For of my life I must a riddle tell.
Toward Auroras Court a nymph doth dwell,
Rich in all beauties which mans eye can see;
Beauties so farre from reach of words that we
Abase her praise saying she doth excell;
Rich in the treasure of deseru'd renowne,
Rich in the riches of a royall heart,
Rich in those gifts which giue th'eternall crowne;
Who, though most rich in these and eu'ry part
Which make the patents of true worldy blisse,
Hath no misfortune but that Rich she is.

XXXVIII

This night, while sleepe begins with heauy wings
To hatch mine eyes, and that vnbitted thought
Doth fall to stray, and my chief powres are brought
To leaue the scepter of all subiect things;
The first that straight my fancys errour brings
Vnto my mind is Stellas image, wrought

19

By Loues own selfe, but with so curious drought
That she, methinks, not onley shines but sings.
I start, look, hearke: but in what closde–vp sence
Was held, in opend sense it flies away,
Leauing me nought but wayling eloquence.
I, seeing better sights in sights decay,
Cald it anew, and wooed Sleepe again;
But him, her host, that vnkind guest had slain.

XXXIX

Come, Sleepe! O Sleepe, the certaine knot of peace,
The baiting–place of wit, the balme of woe,
The poor mans wealth, the prisoners release,
Th' indifferent iudge betweene the high and low!
With shield of proofe shield me from out the prease
Of those fierce darts Despaire at me doth throw.
O make in me those ciuil wars to cease;
I will good tribute pay, if thou do so.
Take thou of me smooth pillowes, sweetest bed,
A chamber deafe of noise and blind of light,
A rosie garland and a weary hed:
And if these things, as being thine in right,
Moue not thy heauy grace, thou shalt in me,
Liuelier then else–where, Stellaes image see.

XL

As good to write, as for to lie and grone.
O Stella deare, how much thy powre hath wrought,
That hast my mind (now of the basest) brought
My still–kept course, while others sleepe, to mone!
Alas, if from the height of Vertues throne
Thou canst vouchsafe the influence of a thought

Vpon a wretch that long thy grace hath sought,
Weigh then how I by thee am ouerthrowne,
And then thinke thus: although thy beautie be
Made manifest by such a victorie,
Yet noble conquerours do wreckes auoid.
Since then thou hast so farre subdued me
That in my heart I offer still to thee,
O do not let thy temple be destroyd!

XLI

Hauing this day my horse, my hand, my launce
Guided so well that I obtain'd the prize,
Both by the iudgement of the English eyes
And of some sent from that sweet enemy Fraunce;
Horsemen my skill in horsemanship aduaunce,
Towne folkes my strength; a daintier iudge applies
His praise to sleight which from good vse doth rise;
Some luckie wits impute it but to chance;
Others, because of both sides I doe take
My blood from them who did excell in this,
Thinke Nature me a man−at−armes did make.
How farre they shot awrie! The true cause is,
Stella lookt on, and from her heau'nly face
Sent forth the beames which made so faire my race.

XLII

O eyes, which do the spheres of beauty moue;
Whose beames be ioyes, whose ioyes all vertues be,
Who, while they make Loue conquer, conquer Loue;
The schooles where Venus hath learnd chastitie:
O eyes, where humble lookes most glorious proue,
Onely lou'd Tyrans, iust in cruelty,

Do not, O doe not, from poore me remoue:
Keep still my zenith, euer shine on me;
For though I neuer see them, but straightwayes
My life forgets to nourish languisht sprites,
Yet still on me, O eyes, dart down your rayes!
And if from majestie of sacred lights
Oppressing mortal sense my death proceed,
Wraceks triumphs be which Loue hie set doth breed.

XLIII

Faire eyes, sweet lips, dear heart, that foolish I
Could hope, by Cupids help, on you to pray,
Since to himselfe he doth your gifts apply,
As his maine force, choise sport, and easefull stay!
For when he will see who dare him gain–say,
Then with those eyes he looeks: lo, by and by
Each soule doth at Loues feet his weapons lay,
Glad if for her he giue them leaue to die.
When he will play, then in her lips he is,
Where, blushing red, that Loues selfe them doe loue,
With either lip he doth the other kisse;
But when he will, for quiets sake, remoue
From all the world, her heart is then his rome,
Where well he knowes no man to him can come.

XLIV

My words I know do well set forth my minde;
My mind bemones his sense of inward smart;
Such smart may pitie claim of any hart;
Her heart, sweet heart, is of no tygres kind:
And yet she heares and yet no pitie I find,
But more I cry, less grace she doth impart.

22

Alas, what cause is there so ouerthwart
That Nobleness it selfe makes thus vnkind?
I much do ghesse, yet finde no truth saue this,
That when the breath of my complaints doth tuch
Those dainty doors vnto the Court of Blisse,
The heau'nly nature of that place is such,
That, once come there, the sobs of mine annoyes
Are metamorphos'd straight to tunes of ioyes.

XLV

Stella oft sees the very face of wo
Painted in my beclowded stormie face,
But cannot skill to pitie my disgrace,
Not though thereof the cause herself she know:
Yet, hearing late a fable which did show
Of louers neuer knowne, a grieuous case,
Pitie thereof gate in her breast such place,
That, from that sea deriu'd, teares spring did flow.
Alas, if Fancie, drawne by imag'd things
Though false, yet with free scope, more grace doth breed
Than seruants wracke, where new doubts honour brings;
Then thinke, my deare, that you in me do reed
Of louers ruine some thrise–sad tragedie.
I am not I: pitie the tale of me.

XLVI

I curst thee oft, I pitie now thy case,
Blind–hitting Boy, since she that thee and me
Rules with a becke, so tyranniseth thee,
That thou must want or food or dwelling–place,
For she protests to banish thee her face.
Her face! O Loue, a roge thou then shouldst be,

If Loue learne not alone to loue and see,
Without desire to feed of further grace.
Alas, poor wag, that now a scholler art
To such a schoolmistresse, whose lessons new
Thou needs must misse, and so thou needs must smart.
Yet, deare, let me his pardon get of you,
So long, though he from book myche to desire,
Till without fewell you can make hot fire.

XLVII

What, haue I thus betray'd my libertie?
Can those blacke beames such burning markes engraue
In my free side, or am I borne a slaue,
Whose necke becomes such yoke of tyrannie?
Or want I sense to feel my misery,
Or sprite, disdaine of such disdaine to haue,
Who for long faith, tho' daily helpe I craue,
May get no almes, but scorne of beggarie.
Vertue, awake! Beautie but beautie is;
I may, I must, I can, I will, I do
Leaue following that which it is gain to misse.
Let her goe! Soft, but here she comes! Goe to,
Vnkind, I loue you not! O me, that eye
Doth make my heart to giue my tongue the lie!

XLVIII

Soules ioy, bend not those morning starres from me
Where Vertue is made strong by Beauties might;
Where Loue is chasteness, Paine doth learn delight,
And Humbleness growes one with Maiesty.
Whateuer may ensue, O let me be
Copartner of the riches of that sight.

Let not mine eyes be hel–driu'n from that light;
O look, O shine, O let me die, and see.
For though I oft myself of them bemone
That through my heart their beamie darts be gone,
Whose cureless wounds euen now most freshly bleed,
Yet since my death–wound is already got,
Deere killer, spare not thy sweete–cruell shot:
A kinde of grace it is to slaye with speed.

XLIX

I on my horse, and Loue on me, doth trie
Our horsemanships, while by strange worke I proue
A horsman to my horse, a horse to Loue,
And now mans wrongs in me, poor beast! descrie.
The raines wherewith my rider doth me tie
Are humbled thoughts, which bit of reuerence moue,
Curb'd–in with feare, but with gilt bosse aboue
Of hope, which makes it seem fair to the eye:
The wand is will; thou, Fancie, saddle art,
Girt fast by Memorie; and while I spurre
My horse, he spurres with sharpe desire my hart.
He sits me fast, howeuer I do sturre,
And now hath made me to his hand so right,
That in the manage my selfe take delight.

L

Stella, the fullnesse of my thoughts of thee
Cannot be staid within my panting breast,
But they do swell and struggle forth of me,
Till that in words thy figure be exprest:
And yet, as soone as they so formed be,
According to my lord Loues oene behest,

25

With sad eies I their weak proportion see
To portrait that which in this world is best.
So that I cannot chuse but write my mind,
And cannot chuse but put out what I write,
While these poor babes their death in birth do find;
And now my pen these lines had dashed quite
But that they stopt his fury from the same,
Because their forefront bare sweet Stellas name.

LI

Pardon mine ears, both I and they do pray,
So may your tongue still flauntingly proceed
To them that do such entertainment need,
So may you still haue somewhat new to say.
On silly me do not the burthen lay
Of all the graue conceits your braine doth breed,
But find some Hercules to beare, insteed
Of Atlas tyrd, your wisedoms heau'nly sway.
For me, while you discourse of courtly tides,
Of cunningest fishers in most troubled streames,
Of straying waies, when valiant Errour guides,
Meanewhile my heart confers with Stellas beames,
And is e'en woe that so sweet comedie
By such vnsuted speech should hindred be.

LII

A strife is growne between Vertue and Loue,
While each pretends that Stella must be his:
Her eyes, her lips, her all, saith Loue, do this,
Since they do weare his badge, most firmly proue.
But Virtue thus that title doth disproue,
That Stella (O dear name!) that Stella is

That vertuous soule, sure heire of heau'nly blisse.
Not this faire outside, which our heart doth moue.
And therefore, though her beautie and her grace
Be Loues indeed, in Stellas selfe he may
By no pretence claime any manner place.
Well, Loue, since this demurre our sute doth stay,
Let Vertue haue that Stellaes selfe, yet thus,
That Vertue but that body graunt to vs.

LIII

In martiall sports I had my cunning tride,
And yet to breake more staues did mee addresse,
While, with the peoples shouts, I must confesse,
Youth, lucke, and praise euen fil'd my veines with pride;
When Cupid, hauing me, his slaue, descride
In Marses livery prauncing in the presse,
What now, Sir Foole! said he, (I would no lesse:)
Looke here, I say! I look'd, and Stella spide,
Who, hard by, made a window send forth light.
My heart then quak'd, then dazled were mine eyes,
One hand forgat to rule, th'other to fight,
Nor trumpets sound I heard, nor friendly cries:
My foe came on, and beate the air for me,
Till that her blush taught me my shame to see.

LIV

Because I breathe not loue to euery one,
Nor doe not vse sette colours for to weare,
Nor nourish speciall locks of vowed haire,
Nor giue each speech a full point of a grone,
The Courtly Nymphes, acquainted with the mone
Of them wich in their lips Loues Standard beare:

What, he! (say they of me): now I dare sweare
He cannot loue; no,no, let him alone.
And thinke so still, so Stella know my minde;
Profess in deede I do not Cupids art;
But you, fair maides, at length this true shall find,
That his right badge is but worne in the hart:
Dumbe Swans, not chattering Pyes, do louers proue;
They loue indeed who quake to say they loue.

LV

Muses, I oft inuoked your holy ayde,
With choisest flowers my speech t' engarland so,
That it, despisde, in true but naked shew
Might winne some grace in your sweet grace arraid;
And oft whole troupes of saddest words I staid,
Striuing abroad a–foraging to go,
Vntill by your inspiring I might know
How their blacke banner might be best displaid.
But now I meane no more your helpe to try,
Nor other sugring of my speech to proue,
But on her name incessantly to cry;
For let me but name her whom I doe loue,
So sweet sounds straight mine eare and heart do hit,
That I well finde no eloquence like it.

LVI

Fy, schoole of Patience, fy! your Lesson is
Far, far too long to learne it without booke:
What, a whole weeke without one peece of looke,
And thinke I should not your large precepts misse!
When I might reade those Letters faire of blisse
Which in her face teach vertue, I could brooke

Somwhat thy leaden counsels, which I tooke
As of a friend that meant not much amisse.
But now that I, alas, doe want her sight,
What, dost thou thinke that I can euer take
In thy cold stuffe a flegmatike delight?
No, Patience; if thou wilt my good, then make
Her come and heare with patience my desire,
And then with patience bid me beare my fire.

LVII

Who hauing made, with many fights, his owne
Each sence of mine, each gift, each pow'r of mind;
Growne now his slaues, he forst them out to find
The thorowest words fit for Woes selfe to grone,
Hoping that when they might finde Stella alone,
Before she could prepare to be vnkind,
Her soule, arm'd but with such a dainty rind,
Should soone be pierc'd with sharpnesse of the mone.
She heard my plaints, and did not onely heare,
But them, so sweet is she, most sweetly sing,
With that faire breast making Woes darknesse cleare.
A pretie case; I hoped her to bring
To feele my griefe; and she, with face and voyce,
So sweets my paines that my paines me reioyce.

LVIII

Doubt there hath beene when with his golden chaine
The orator so farre mens hearts doth bind,
That no pace else their guided steps can find
But as he them more short or slack doth raine;
Whether with words this soueraignty he gaine,
Cloth'd with fine tropes, with strongest reasons lin'd,

Or else pronouncing grace, wherewith his mind
Prints his owne liuely forme in rudest braine.
Now iudge by this: in piercing phrases late
Th' Anatomie of all my woes I wrate;
Stellas sweet breath the same to me did reed.
O voyce, O face! maugre my speeches might,
Which wooed wo, most rauishing delight
Euen those sad words euen in sad me did breed.

LIX

Deere, why make you more of a dog then me?
If he doe loue, I burne, I burne in loue;
If he waite well, I neuer thence would moue;
If he be faire, yet but a dog can be;
Little he is, so little worth is he;
He barks, my songs thine owne voyce oft doth proue;
Bidden, perhaps he fetched thee a gloue,
But I, vnbid, fetch euen my soule to thee.
Yet, while I languish, him that bosome clips,
That lap doth lap, nay lets, in spite of spite,
This sowre—breath'd mate taste of those sugred lips.
Alas, if you graunt onely such delight
To witlesse things, then Loue, I hope (since wit
Becomes a clog) will soone ease me of it.

LX

When my good Angell guides me to the place
Where all my good I doe in Stella see,
That heau'n of ioyes throwes onely downe on me
Thundring disdaines and lightnings of disgrace;
But when the ruggedst step of Fortunes race
Makes me fall from her sight, then sweetly she,

With words wherein the Muses treasures be,
Shewes loue and pitie to my absent case.
Now I, wit–beaten long by hardest fate,
So dull am, that I cannot looke into
The ground of this fierce loue and louely hate.
Then, some good body, tell me how I do,
Whose presence absence, absence presence is;
Blest in my curse, and cursed in my blisse.

LXI

Oft with true sighs, oft with vncalled teares,
Now with slow words, now with dumbe eloquence,
I Stellas eyes assaid, inuade her eares;
But this, at last, is her sweet breath'd defence:
That who indeed in–felt affection beares,
So captiues to his Saint both soule and sence,
That, wholly hers, all selfenesse he forbeares,
Then his desires he learnes, his liues course thence.
Now, since her chast mind hates this loue in me,
With chastned mind I straight must shew that she
Shall quickly me from what she hates remoue.
O Doctor Cupid, thou for me reply;
Driu'n else to graunt, by Angels Sophistrie,
That I loue not without I leaue to loue.

LXII

Late tyr'd with wo, euen ready for to pine
With rage of loue, I cald my Loue vnkind;
She in whose eyes loue, though vnfelt, doth shine,
Sweet said, that I true loue in her should find.
I ioyed; but straight thus watred was my wine;
That loue she did, but lou'd a loue not blind;

Which would not let me, whom shee lou'd, decline
From nobler course, fit for my birth and mind:
And therefore, by her loues Authority,
Wild me these tempests of vaine loue to flie,
And anchor fast my selfe on Vertues shore.
Alas, if this the only mettall be
Of loue new–coin'd to help my beggary,
Deere, loue me not, that you may loue me more.

LXIII

O grammer–rules, O now your vertues show;
So children still reade you with awfull eyes,
As my young doue may, in your precepts wise,
Her graunt to me by her owne vertue know:
For late, with heart most hie, with eyes most lowe,
I crau'd the thing which euer she denies;
Shee, lightning loue, displaying Venus skies,
Least once should not be heard, twise said, No, no.
Sing then, my Muse, now Io Pæn sing;
Heau'ns enuy not at my high triumphing,
But grammers force with sweete successe confirme:
For grammer says, (O this, deare Stella , say,)
For grammer sayes, (to grammer who sayes nay?)
That in one speech two negatiues affirme!

LXIV

No more, my deare, no more these counsels trie;
O giue my passions leaue to run their race;
Let Fortune lay on me her worst disgrace;
Let folke orecharg'd with braine against me crie;
Let clouds bedimme my face, breake in mine eye;
Let me no steps but of lost labour trace;

Let all the earth with scorne recount my case,
But do not will me from my loue to flie.
I do not enuie Aristotless wit,
Nor do aspire to Cæsars bleeding fame;
Nor ought do care though some aboue me sit;
Nor hope, nor wish another course to frame
But that which once may win thy cruell hart:
Thou art my wit, and thou my vertue art.

LXV

Loue, by sure proofe I may call thee vnkind,
That giu'st no better ear to my iust cries;
Thou whom to me such good turnes should bind,
As I may well recount, but none can prize:
For when, nak'd Boy, thou couldst no harbour finde
In this old world, growne now so too, too wise,
I lodgd thee in my heart, and being blind
By nature borne, I gaue to thee mine eyes;
Mine eyes! my light, my heart, my life, alas!
If so great seruices may scorned be,
Yet let this thought thy Tygrish courage passe,
That I perhaps am somewhat kinne to thee;
Since in thine armes, if learnd fame truth hath spread,
Thou bear'st the Arrow, I the Arrow–head.

LXVI

And do I see some cause a hope to feede,
Or doth the tedious burden of long wo
In weaken'd minds quick apprehending breed
Of euerie image which may comfort shew?
I cannot brag of word, much lesse of deed,
Fortune wheeles still with me in one sort slow;
My wealth no more, and no whit lesse my need;

Desier still on stilts of Feare doth go.
And yet amid all feares a hope there is,
Stolne to my hart since last faire night, nay day,
Stellas eyes sent to me the beames of blisse,
Looking on me while I lookt other way:
But when mine eyes backe to their heau'n did moue,
They fled with blush which guiltie seem'd of loue.

LXVII

Hope, art thou true, or doest thou flatter me?
Doth Stella now beginne with piteous eye
The ruines of her conquest to espie?
Will she take time before all wracked be?
Her eyes–speech is translated thus by thee,
But failst thou not in phrases so heau'nly hye?
Looke on againe, the faire text better prie;
What blushing notes dost thou in Margent see?
What sighes stolne out, or kild before full–borne?
Hast thou found such and such–like arguments,
Or art thou else to comfort me forsworne?
Well, how–so thou interpret the contents,
I am resolu'd thy errour to maintaine,
Rather then by more truth to get more paine.

LXVIII

Stella, the onely planet of my light,
Light of my life, and life of my desire,
Chiefe good whereto my hope doth only aspire,
World of my wealth, and heau'n of my delight;
Why dost thou spend the treasures of thy sprite
With voice more fit to wed Amphions lyre,
Seeking to quench in me the noble fire

34

Fed by thy worth, and kindled by thy sight?
And all in vaine: for while thy breath most sweet
With choisest words, thy words with reasons rare,
Thy reasons firmly set on Vertues feet,
Labour to kill in me this killing care:
O thinke I then, what paradise of ioy
It is, so faire a vertue to enioy!

LXIX

O ioy to high for my low stile to show!
O blisse fit for a nobler seat then me!
Enuie, put out thine eyes, least thou do see
What oceans of delight in me do flowe!
My friend, that oft saw through all maskes my wo,
Come, come, and let me powre my selfe on thee.
Gone is the Winter of my miserie!
My Spring appeares; O see what here doth grow:
For Stella hath, with words where faith doth shine,
Of her high heart giu'n me the Monarchie:
I, I, O I, may say that she is mine!
And though she giue but thus conditionly,
This realme of blisse while vertuous course I take,
No kings be crown'd but they some couenants make.

LXX

My Muse may well grudge at my heau'nly ioy,
Yf still I force her in sad rimes to creepe:
She oft hath drunk my teares, now hopes to enioy
Nectar of mirth, since I Ioues cup do keepe.
Sonets be not bound Prentice to annoy;
Trebles sing high, so well as bases deepe;
Griefe but Loues winter–liuerie is; the boy

Hath cheekes to smile, so well as eyes to weepe.
Come then, my Muse, shew thou height of delight
In well–raisde notes; my pen, the best it may,
Shall paint out ioy, though in but blacke and white.
Cease, eager Muse; peace, pen, for my sake stay,
I giue you here my hand for truth of this,
Wise silence is best musicke vnto blisse.

LXXI

Who will in fairest booke of Nature know
How vertue may best lodg'd in Beautie be,
Let him but learne of Loue to reade in thee,
Stella, those faire lines which true goodnesse show.
There shall he find all vices ouerthrow,
Not by rude force, but sweetest soueraigntie
Of reason, from whose light those night–birds flie,
That inward sunne in thine eyes shineth so.
And, not content to be Perfections heire
Thy selfe, doest striue all minds that way to moue,
Who marke in thee what is in thee most faire:
So while thy beautie drawes the heart to loue,
As fast thy vertue bends that loue to good:
But, ah, Desire still cries, Giue me some food.

LXXII

Desire, though thou my old companion art,
And oft so clings to my pure loue that I
One from the other scarcely can discrie,
While each doth blowe the fier of my hart;
Now from thy fellowship I needs must part;
Venus is taught with Dians wings to flie;
I must no more in thy sweet passions lie;

Vertues gold must now head my Cupids dart.
Seruice and honour, wonder with delight,
Feare to offend, will worthie to appeare,
Care shining in mine eyes, faith in my sprite;
These things are left me by my onely Deare:
But thou, Desire, because thou wouldst haue all,
Now banisht art; but yet, alas, how shall?

LXXIII

Loue, still a Boy, and oft a wanton is,
School'd onely by his mothers tender eye;
What wonder then if he his lesson misse,
When for so soft a rodde deare play he trye?
And yet my Starre, because a sugred kisse
In sport I suckt while she asleepe did lye,
Doth lowre, nay chide, nay threat for only this.
Sweet, it was saucie Loue, not humble I.
But no scuse serues; she makes her wrath appeare
In beauties throne: see now, who dares come neare
Those scarlet Iudges, thretning bloudie paine.
O heau'nly foole, thy most kisse—worthy face
Anger inuests with such a louely grace,
That Angers selfe I needs must kisse againe.

LXXIV

I neuer dranke of Aganippe well,
Nor euer did in shade of Tempe sit,
And Muses scorne with vulgar brains to dwell;
Poore Layman I, for sacred rites vnfit.
Some doe I heare of Poets fury tell,
But, God wot, wot not what they meane by it;
And this I sweare by blackest brooke of hell,

I am no pick–purse of anothers wit.
How falles it then, that with so smooth an ease
My thoughts I speake; and what I speake doth flow
In verse, and that my verse best wits doth please?
Ghesse we the cause? What, is it this? Fie, no.
Or so? Much lesse. How then? Sure thus it is,
My lips are sweet, inspir'd with Stellas kisse.

LXXV

Of all the Kings that euer here did raigne,
Edward, nam'd fourth, as first in praise I name:
Not for his faire outside, nor well–lin'd braine,
Although lesse gifts impe feathers oft on fame.
Nor that he could, young–wise, wise–valiant, frame
His sires reuenge, ioyn'd with a kingdomes gaine;
And gain'd by Mars, could yet mad Mars so tame,
That balance weigh'd, what sword did late obtaine.
Nor that he made the floure–de–luce so 'fraid,
(Though strongly hedg'd) of bloudy lyons pawes,
That wittie Lewes to him a tribute paid:
Nor this, nor that, nor any such small cause;
But only for this worthy King durst proue
To lose his crowne, rather than faile his loue.

LXXVI

She comes, and streight therewith her shining twins do moue
Their rayes to me, who in their tedious absence lay
Benighted in cold wo; but now appears my day,
The only light of ioy, the only warmth of loue.
She comes with light and warmth, which, like Aurora, proue
Of gentle force, so that mine eyes dare gladly play
With such a rosie Morne, whose beames, most freshly gay,

38

Scorch not, but onely doe dark chilling sprites remoue.
But lo, while I do speake, it groweth noone with me,
Her flamie–glistring lights increse with time and place,
My heart cries, oh! it burnes, mine eyes now dazl'd be;
No wind, no shade can coole: what helpe then in my case?
But with short breath, long looks, staid feet, and aching hed,
Pray that my Sunne goe downe with meeker beames to bed.

LXXVII

Those lookes, whose beames be ioy, whose motion is delight;
That face, whose lecture shews what perfect beauty is;
That presence, which doth giue darke hearts a liuing light;
That grace, which Venus weeps that she her selfe doth misse;
That hand, which without touch holds more then Atlas might;
Those lips, which make deaths pay a meane price for a kisse;
That skin, whose passe–praise hue scornes this poor tearm of white;
Those words, which do sublime the quintessence of bliss;
That voyce, which makes the soule plant himselfe in the ears,
That conuersation sweet, where such high comforts be,
As, consterd in true speech, the name of heaun it beares;
Makes me in my best thoughts and quietst iudgments see
That in no more but these I might be fully blest:
Yet, ah, my mayd'n Muse doth blush to tell the best.

LXXVIII

O how the pleasant ayres of true loue be
Infected by those vapours which arise
From out that noysome gulfe, which gaping lies
Betweene the iawes of hellish Ielousie!
A monster, others harme, selfe–miserie,
Beauties plague, Vertues scourge, succour of lies;
Who his owne ioy to his owne hurt applies,

And onely cherish doth with iniurie:
Who since he hath, by Natures speciall grace,
So piercing pawes as spoyle when they embrace;
So nimble feet as stirre still, though on thornes;
So many eyes, ay seeking their owne woe;
So ample eares as neuer good newes know:
Is it not euill that such a deuil wants hornes?

LXXIX

Sweet kisse, thy sweets I faine would sweetly endite,
Which, euen of sweetnesse sweetest sweetner art;
Pleasingst consort, where each sence holds a part;
Which, coupling Doues, guides Venus chariot right.
Best charge, and brauest retrait in Cupids fight;
A double key, which opens to the heart,
Most rich when most riches it impart;
Nest of young ioyes, Schoolemaster of delight,
Teaching the meane at once to take and giue;
The friendly fray, where blowes both wound and heale,
The prettie death, while each in other liue.
Poore hopes first wealth, ostage of promist weale;
Breakfast of loue. But lo, lo, where she is,
Cease we to praise; now pray we for a kisse.

LXXX

Sweet–swelling lip, well maist thou swell in pride,
Since best wits thinke it wit thee to admire;
Natures praise, Vertues stall; Cupids cold fire,
Whence words, not words but heau'nly graces slide;
The new Parnassus, where the Muses bide;
Sweetner of Musicke, Wisedomes beautifier,
Breather of life, and fastner of desire,

40

Where Beauties blush in Honors graine is dide.
Thus much my heart compeld my mouth to say;
But now, spite of my heart, my mouth will stay,
Loathing all lies, doubting this flatterie is:
And no spurre can his resty race renewe,
Without, how farre this praise is short of you,
Sweet Lipp, you teach my mouth with one sweet kisse.

LXXXI

O kisse, which dost those ruddie gemmes impart,
Or gemmes or fruits of new−found Paradise,
Breathing all blisse, and sweetning to the heart,
Teaching dumbe lips a nobler exercise;
O kisse, which soules, euen soules, together ties
By linkes of loue and only Natures art,
How faine would I paint thee to all mens eyes.
Or of thy gifts at least shade out some part!
But she forbids; with blushing words she sayes
She builds her fame on higher−seated praise.
But my heart burnes; I cannot silent be.
Then, since, dear life, you faine would haue me peace,
And I, mad with delight, want wit to cease,
Stop you my mouth with still still kissing me.

LXXXII

Nymph of the garden where all beauties be,
Beauties which do in excellencie passe
His who till death lookt in a watrie glasse,
Or hers whom nakd the Troian boy did see;
Sweet−gard'n−nymph, which keepes the Cherrie−tree
Whose fruit doth farre the Hesperian tast surpasse,
Most sweet−faire, most faire−sweete, do not, alas,

From comming neare those Cherries banish mee.
For though, full of desire, empty of wit,
Admitted late by your best–graced grace,
I caught at one of them, and hungry bit;
Pardon that fault; once more grant me the place;
And I do sweare, euen by the same delight,
I will but kisse; I neuer more will bite.

LXXXIII

Good brother Philip, I haue borne you long;
I was content you should in fauour creepe,
While craftely you seem'd your cut to keepe,
As though that faire soft hand did you great wrong:
I bare with enuie, yet I bare your song,
When in her necke you did loue–ditties peepe;
Nay (more foole I) oft suffred you to sleepe
In lillies neast where Loues selfe lies along.
What, doth high place ambitious thoughts augment?
Is sawcinesse reward of curtesie?
Cannot such grace your silly selfe content,
But you must needs with those lips billing be,
And through those lips drinke nectar from that toong?
Leaue that, Syr Phip, least off your neck be wroong!

LXXXIV

High way, since you my chiefe Pernassus be,
And that my Muse, to some eares not vnsweet,
Tempers her words to trampling horses feete
More oft then to a chamber–melodie.
Now, blessed you beare onward blessed me
To her, where I my heart, safe–left, shall meet;
My Muse and I must you of dutie greet

With thankes and wishes, wishing thankfully.
Be you still faire, honord by publicke heede;
By no encroachment wrong'd, nor time forgot;
Nor blam'd for bloud, nor sham'd for sinfull deed;
And that you know I enuy you no lot
Of highest wish, I wish you so much bliss,
Hundreds of yeares you Stellaes feet may kisse.

LXXXV

I see the house, (my heart thy selfe containe!)
Beware full sailes drowne not thy tottring barge,
Least ioy, by nature apt sprites to enlarge,
Thee to thy wracke beyond thy limits straine;
Nor do like Lords whose weake confused braine
Not 'pointing to fit folkes each vndercharge,
While euerie office themselues will discharge,
With doing all, leaue nothing done but paine.
But giue apt seruants their due place: let eyes
See beauties totall summe summ'd in her face;
Let eares heare speach which wit to wonder ties;
Let breath sucke vp those sweetes; let armes embrace
The globe of weale, lips Loues indentures make;
Thou but of all the kingly tribute take.

LXXXVI

Alas, whence came this change of lookes? If I
Haue chang'd desert, let mine owne conscience be
A still−felt plague to selfe−condemning mee;
Let woe gripe on my heart, shame loade mine eye:
But if all faith, like spotlesse Ermine, ly
Safe in my soule, which only doth to thee,
As his sole obiect of felicitie,

With wings of loue in aire of wonder flie,
O ease your hand, treate not so hard your slaue;
In iustice paines come not till faults do call:
Or if I needs, sweet Iudge, must torments haue,
Vse something else to chasten me withall
Then those blest eyes, where all my hopes do dwell:
No doome should make ones Heau'n become his Hell.

LXXXVII

When I was forst from Stella euer deere,
Stella, food of my thoughts, hart of my hart;
Stella, whose eyes make all my tempests cleere,
By Stellas lawes of duetie to depart;
Alas, I found that she with me did smart;
I saw that teares did in her eyes appeare;
I sawe that sighes her sweetest lips did part,
And her sad words my sadded sense did heare.
For me, I wept to see pearles scatter'd so;
I sigh'd her sighes, and wailed for her wo;
Yet swam in ioy, such loue in her was seene.
Thus, while th' effect most bitter was to me,
And nothing then the cause more sweet could be,
I had bene vext, if vext I had not beene.

LXXXVIII

Out, traytor Absence, dar'st thou counsell me
From my deare captainesse to run away,
Because in braue array heere marcheth she,
That, to win mee, oft shewes a present pay?
Is faith so weake? or is such force in thee?
When sun is hid, can starres such beames display?
Cannot heau'ns food, once felt, keepe stomakes free

From base desire on earthly cates to pray?
Tush, Absence; while thy mistes eclipse that light,
My orphan sense flies to the inward sight,
Where memory sets forth the beames of loue;
That, where before hart lou'd and eyes did see,
In hart both sight and loue now coupled be:
Vnited pow'rs make each the stronger proue.

LXXXIX

Now that of absence the most irksom night
With darkest shade doth ouercome my day;
Since Stellaes eyes, wont to giue me my day,
Leauing my hemisphere, leaue me in night;
Each day seemes long, and longs for long–staid night;
The night, as tedious, wooes th' approch of day:
Tired with the dusty toiles of busie day,
Languisht with horrors of the silent night,
Suff'ring the euils both of day and night,
While no night is more darke then is my day,
Nor no day hath lesse quiet then my night:
With such bad–mixture of my night and day,
That liuing thus in blackest Winter night,
I feele the flames of hottest Sommer day.

XC

Stella, thinke not that I by verse seeke fame,
Who seeke, who hope, who loue, who liue but thee;
Thine eyes my pride, thy lips mine history:
If thou praise not, all other praise is shame.
Nor so ambitious am I, as to frame
A nest for my young praise in lawrell tree:
In truth, I sweare I wish not there should be

Grau'd in my epitaph a Poets name.
Ne, if I would, could I iust title make,
That any laud thereof to me should growe,
Without my plumes from others wings I take:
For nothing from my wit or will doth flow,
Since all my words thy beauty doth endite,
And Loue doth hold my hand, and makes me write.

XCI

Stella, while now, by Honours cruell might,
I am from you, light of my life, misled,
And whiles, faire you, my sunne, thus ouerspred
With Absence vaile, I liue in Sorrowes night;
If this darke place yet shewe like candle–light,
Some beauties peece, as amber–colour'd hed,
Milke hands, rose cheeks, or lips more sweet, more red;
Or seeing jets blacke but in blacknesse bright;
They please, I do confesse they please mine eyes.
But why? because of you they models be;
Models, such be wood–globes of glist'ring skies.
Deere therefore be not iaelous ouer me,
If you heare that they seeme my heart to moue;
Not them, O no, but you in them I loue.

XCII

Be your words made, good Sir, of Indian ware,
That you allow me them by so small rate?
Or do you curtted Spartanes imitate?
Or do you meane my tender eares to spare,
That to my questions you so totall are?
When I demaund of Phoenix–Stellas state,
You say, forsooth, you left her well of late:

46

O God, thinke you that satisfies my care?
I would know whether she did sit or walke;
How cloth'd; how waited on; sigh'd she, or smilde
Whereof, with whom, how often did she talke;
With what pastimes Times iourney she beguilde;
If her lips daignd to sweeten my poore name.
Saie all; and all well sayd, still say the same.

XCIII

O fate, O fault, O curse, child of my blisse!
What sobs can giue words grace my griefe to show?
What inke is blacke inough to paint my woe?
Through me (wretch me) euen Stella vexed is.
Yet, Trueth, if Caitives breath may call thee, this
Witnesse with me, that my foule stumbling so,
From carelessenesse did in no maner grow;
But wit, confus'd with too much care, did misse.
And do I, then, my selfe this vaine scuse giue?
I haue (liue I, and know this) harmed thee;
Tho' worlds 'quite me, shall I my selfe forgiue?
Only with paines my paines thus eased be,
That all thy hurts in my harts wracke I reede;
I cry thy sighs, my deere, thy teares I bleede.

XCIV

Griefe, find the words; for thou hast made my braine
So darke with misty vapuors, which arise
From out thy heauy mould, that inbent eyes
Can scarce discerne the shape of mine owne paine.
Do thou, then (for thou canst) do thou complaine
For my poore soule, which now that sicknesse tries,
Which euen to sence, sence of it selfe denies,

Though harbengers of death lodge there his traine.
Or if thy loue of plaint yet mine forbeares,
As of a Caitife worthy so to die;
Yet waile thy selfe, and waile with causefull teares,
That though in wretchednesse thy life doth lie,
Yet growest more wretched then by nature beares
By being plac'd in such a wretch as I.

XCV

Yet sighes, deare sighs, indeede true friends you are,
That do not leaue your best friend at the wurst,
But, as you with my breast I oft haue nurst,
So, gratefull now, you waite vpon my care.
Faint coward Ioy no longer tarry dare,
Seeing Hope yeeld when this wo strake him furst;
Delight exclaims he is for my fault curst,
Though oft himselfe my mate in Armes he sware;
Nay, Sorrow comes with such maine rage, that he
Kils his owne children (teares) finding that they
By Loue were made apt to consort with me.
Only, true Sighs, you do not goe away:
Thanke may you haue for such a thankfull part,
Thank—worthiest yet when you shall break my hart.

XCVI

Thought, with good cause thou lik'st so well the night,
Since kind or chance giues both one liuerie,
Both sadly blacke, both blackly darkned be;
Night bard from Sunne, thou from thy owne sunlight;
Silence in both displaies his sullen might;
Slow heauinesse in both holds one degree
That full of doubts, thou of perplexity;

48

Thy teares expresse Nights natiue moisture right;
In both amazeful solitarinesse:
In night, of sprites, the gastly powers do stur;
In thee or sprites or sprited gastlinesse.
But, but (alas) Nights side the ods hath fur:
For that, at length, yet doth inuite some rest;
Thou, though still tired, yet still doost it detest.

XCVII

Dian, that faine would cheare her friend the Night,
Shewes her oft, at the full, her fairest face,
Bringing with her those starry Nymphs, whose chace
From heau'nly standing hits each mortall wight.
But ah, poore Night, in loue with Phoebus light,
And endlesly dispairing of his grace,
Her selfe, to shewe no other ioy hath place;
Sylent and sad, in mourning weedes doth dight.
Euen so (alas) a lady, Dians peere,
With choise delights and rarest company
Would faine driue cloudes from out my heauy cheere;
But, wo is me, though Ioy her selfe were she,
Shee could not shew my blind braine waies of ioy,
While I despaire my sunnes sight to enioy.

XCVIII

Ah, bed! the field where Ioyes peace some do see,
The field where all my thoughts to warre be train'd,
How is thy grace by my strange fortune strain'd!
How thy lee−shores by my sighes stormed be!
With sweete soft shades thou oft inuitest me
To steale some rest; but, wretch, I am constrain'd,
Spurd with Loues spur, though gald, and shortly rain'd

With Cares hard hand to turne and tosse in thee,
While the blacke horrors of the silent night
Paint Woes blacke face so liuely to my sight
That tedious leasure markes each wrinkled line:
But when Aurora leades out Phoebus daunce,
Mine eyes then only winke; for spite, perchaunce,
That wormes should haue their sun, &I want mine.

XCIX

When far–spent Night perswades each mortall eye,
To whome nor Art nor Nature graunteth light,
To lay his then marke–wanting shafts of sight,
Clos'd with their quiuers, in Sleeps armory;
With windowes ope, then most my mind doth lie,
Viewing the shape of darknesse, and delight
Takes in that sad hue, which, with th' inward night
Of his mazde powers, keepes perfet harmony:
But when birds charme, and that sweete aire which is
Mornes messenger, with rose–enameld skies
Cals each wight to salute the floure of blisse;
In tombe of lids then buried are mine eyes,
Forst by their Lord, who is asham'd to find
Such light in sense, with such a darkned mind.

C

O teares! no teares, but raine, from Beauties skies,
Making those lillies and those roses growe,
Which ay most faire, now more then most faire shew,
While gracefull Pitty Beautie beautifies.
O honied sighs! which from that breast do rise,
Whose pants do make vnspilling creame to flow,
Wing'd with whose breath, so pleasing Zephires blow.

As might refresh the hell where my soule fries.
O plaints! conseru'd in such a sugred phrase,
That Eloquence itself enuies your praise,
While sobd–out words a perfect musike giue.
Such teares, sighs, plaints, no sorrow is, but ioy:
Or if such heauenly signes must proue annoy,
All mirth farewell, let me in sorrow liue.

CI

Stella is sicke, and in that sicke–bed lies
Sweetnesse, which breathes and pants as oft as she:
And Grace, sicke too, such fine conclusion tries,
That Sickenesse brags it selfe best grac'd to be.
Beauty is sicke, but sicke in so faire guise,
That in that palenesse Beauties white we see;
And Ioy, which is inseparate from those eyes,
Stella now learnes (strange case) to weepe in me.
Loue mones thy paine, and like a faithfull page,
As thy lookes sturre, runs vp and downe, to make
All folkes prest at thy will thy paine to swage;
Nature with care sweates for hir darlings sake,
Knowing worlds passe, ere she enough can finde,
Of such heauen–stuffe to cloath so heau'nly minde.

CII

Where be those roses gone, which sweetned so our eyes?
Where those red cheeks, which oft, with faire encrease, did frame
The height of honour in the kindly badge of shame?
Who hath the crimson weeds stolne from my morning skies?
How doth the colour vade of those vermilion dies,
Which Nature self did make, and self–ingrain'd the same?
I would know by what right this palenesse ouercame

That hue whose force my hart still vnto thraldome ties?
Galens adoptiue sonnes, who by a beaten way
Their iudgements hackney on, the fault of sicknesse lay;
But feeling proofe makes me say they mistake it furre:
It is but loue which makes this paper perfit white,
To write therein more fresh the storie of delight,
Whiles Beauties reddest inke Venus for him doth sturre.

CIII

O happie Thames, that didst my Stella beare!
I saw thee with full many a smiling line
Vpon thy cheerefull face, Ioyes liuery weare,
While those faire planets on thy streames did shine.
The boate for ioy could not to daunce forbear,
While wanton winds, with beauties so diuine
Ravisht, staid not, till in her golden haire
They did themselues (O sweetest prison) twine.
And faine those Æols youth there would their stay
Haue made, but forst by Nature still to flie,
First did with puffing kisse those Lockes display:
She, so disheuld blusht: from window I
With sight thereof cride out, O faire disgrace,
Let Honor selfe to thee grant highest place.

CIV

Enuious wits, what hath bene mine offence,
That with such poysonous care my lookes you marke,
That to each word, nay sigh of mine, you harke,
As grudging me my sorrowes eloquence?
Ah, is it not enough, that I am thence,
Thence, so farre thence, that scantly any sparke
Of comfort dare come to this dungeon darke,

52

Where Rigours exile lockes vp al my sense?
But if I by a happie window passe,
If I but stars vppon mine armour beare;
Sicke, thirsty, glad (though but of empty glasse):
Your morall notes straight my hid meaning teare
From out my ribs, and, puffing, proues that I
Doe Stella loue: fooles, who doth it deny?

CV

Vnhappie sight, and hath shee vanisht by
So nere, in so good time, so free a place!
Dead Glasse, dost thou thy obiect so imbrace,
As what my hart still sees thou canst not spie!
I sweare by her I loue and lacke, that I
Was not in fault, who bent thy dazling race
Onely vnto the heau'n of Stellas face,
Counting but dust what in the way did lie.
But cease, mine eyes, your teares do witnesse well
That you, guiltlesse thereof, your nectar mist:
Curst be the page from whome the bad torch fell:
Curst be the night which did your strife resist:
Curst be the coachman that did driue so fast,
With no lesse curse then absence makes me tast.

CVI

O absent presence! Stella is not here;
False–flatt'ring hope, that with so faire a face
Bare me in hand, that in this orphane place,
Stella, I say my Stella, should appeare:
What saist thou now? where is that dainty cheere
Thou toldst mine eyes should helpe their famisht case?
But thou art gone, now that selfe–felt disgrace

Doth make me most to wish thy comfort neer.
But heere I do store of faire ladies meet,
Who may with charme of conuersation sweete,
Make in my heauy mould new thoughts to grow.
Sure they preuaile as much with me, as he
That bad his friend, but then new maim'd to be
Mery with him, and so forget his woe.

CVII

Stella, since thou so right a princesse art
Of all the Powers which Life bestowes on me,
That ere by them ought vndertaken be,
They first resort vnto that soueraigne part;
Sweete, for a while giue thy lieutenancie
To this great cause, which needes both use and art.
And as a Queene, who from her presence sends
Whom she employes, dismisse from thee my wit,
Till it haue wrought what thy owne will attends.
On seruants shame oft maisters blame doth sit:
O let not fooles in me thy workes reproue,
And scorning say, See what it is to loue!

CVIII

When Sorrow (vsing mine owne fiers might)
Melts downe his lead into my boyling brest
Through that darke furnace to my hart opprest,
There shines a ioy from thee my only light:
But soone as thought of thee breeds my delight,
And my yong soule flutters to thee his nest,
Most rude Despaire, my daily vnbidden guest,
Clips streight my wings, streight wraps me in his night,
And makes me then bow downe my heade, and say,

Astrophel and Stella

Ah, what doth Phoebus gold that wretch auaile
Whom Iron doores doe keepe from vse of day?
So strangely (alas) thy works on me preuaile,
That in my woes for thee thou art my ioy,
And in my ioyes for thee my onely annoy.
The following two sonnets were added by Grosart as having been intended for the sonnet
cycle, though they did not appear here in the early editions:

CIX

Thou blind mans marke, thou fooles selfe–chosen snare,
Fond fancies scum, and dregs of scatter'd thought:
Band of all euils, cradle of causelesse care;
Thou web of will, whose end is neuer wrought:
Desire! Desire! I haue too dearly bought,
With prise of mangled mind, thy worthlesse ware;
Too long, too long, asleepe thou hast me brought,
Who shouldst my mind to higher things prepare.
But yet in vaine thou hast my ruine sought;
In vaine thou madest me to vaine things aspire;
In vaine thou kindlest all thy smokie fire;
For Vertue hath this better lesson taught,—
Within my selfe to seeke my onelie hire,
Desiring nought but how to kill Desire.

CX

Leaue, me, O loue which reachest but to dust,
And thou, my mind, aspire to higher things.
Grow rich in that which neuer taketh rust;
Whateuer fades, but fading pleasure brings.
Draw in thy beames, and humble all thy might

Astrophel and Stella

To that sweet yoke where lasting freedomes be;
Which breakes the clowdes, and opens forth the light,
That doth both shine and giue us sight to see.
O take fast hold; let that light be thy guide
In this small course which birth drawes out to death,
And thinke how euill becommeth him to slide,
Who seeketh heau'n, and comes of heau'nly breath.
Then farewell world; thy vttermost I see:
Eternall Loue, maintaine thy life in me.
spendidis longum valedico nugis.

Songs

First Song.

Doubt you to whom my Muse these notes entendeth,
Which now my breast, surcharg'd, to musick lendeth!
To you, to you, all song of praise is due,
Only in you my song begins and endeth.

Who hath the eyes which marrie state with pleasure!
Who keeps the key of Natures cheifest treasure!
To you, to you, all song of praise is due,
Only for you the heau'n forgate all measure.

Who hath the lips, where wit in fairnesse raigneth!
Who womankind at once both deckes and stayneth!
To you, to you, all song of praise is due,
Onely by you Cupid his crowne maintaineth.

Who hath the feet, whose step all sweetnesse planteth!

Astrophel and Stella

Who else, for whom Fame worthy trumpets wanteth!
To you, to you, all song of praise is due,
Onely to you her scepter Venus granteth.

Who hath the breast, whose milk doth patience nourish!
Whose grace is such, that when it chides doth cherish!
To you, to you, all song of praise is due,
Onelie through you the tree of life doth flourish.

Who hath the hand which, without stroke, subdueth!
Who long−dead beautie with increase reneueth!
To you, to you, all song of praise is due,
Onely at you all enuie hopelesse rueth.

Who hath the haire, which, loosest, fastest tieth!
Who makes a man liue, then glad when he dieth!
To you, to you, all song of praise is due,
Only of you the flatterer neuer lieth.

Who hath the voyce, which soule from sences thunders!
Whose force, but yours, the bolts of beautie thunders!
To you, to you, all song of praise is due,
Only with you not miracles are wonders.

Doubt you, to whome my Muse these notes intendeth,
Which now my breast, oercharg'd, to musicke lendeth!
To you, to you, all song of praise is due:
Only in you my song begins and endeth.

Second Song.

Haue I caught my heau'nly iewell,

Astrophel and Stella

Teaching Sleepe most faire to be!
Now will I teach her that she,
When she wakes, is too—too cruell.

Since sweet Sleep her eyes hath charmed,
The two only darts of Loue,
Now will I, with that Boy, proue,
Some play, while he is disamed.

Her tongue, waking, still refuseth,
Giuing frankly niggard no:
Now will I attempt to know
What no her tongue, sleeping, vseth.

See the hand that, waking, gardeth,
Sleeping, grants a free resort:
Now I will inuade the fort,
Cowards Loue with losse rewardeth.

But, O foole, thinke of the danger
Of her iust and high disdaine;
Now will I, alas, refraine;
Loue feares nothing else but anger.

Yet those lips, so sweetly swelling,
Do inuite a stealing kisse.
Now will I but venture this;
Who will reade, must first learne spelling.

Oh, sweet kisse! but ah, shes waking!
Lowring beautie chastens me:
Now will I for feare hence flee;
Foole, more Foole for no more taking.

Astrophel and Stella

Third Song.

If Orpheus voyce had force to breathe such musickes loue
Through pores of senceles trees, as it could make them moue;
If stones good measure daunc'd, the Theban walles to build
To cadence of the tunes which Amphions lyre did yeeld;
More cause a like effect at least—wise bringeth:
O stones, O trees, learne hearing,—Stella singeth.

If loue might sweeten so a boy of shepheard brood,
To make a lyzard dull, to taste loues dainty food;
If eagle fierce could so in Grecian mayde delight,
As her eyes were his light, her death his endlesse night,
Earth gaue that loue; heau'n, I trow, loue refineth,
O birds, O beasts, looke loue (lo) Stella shineth.

The beasts, birds, stones, and trees feele this, and, feeling, loue;
And if the trees nor stones stirre not the same to proue,
Nor beasts nor birds do come vnto this blessed gaze,
Know that small loue is quicke, and great loue doth amaze;
They are amaz'd, but you with reason armed,
O eyes, O eares of men, how you are charmed!

Fourth Song.

Onely Ioy, now here you are,
Fit to heare and ease my care,
Let my whispering voyce obtaine
Sweete reward for sharpest paine;
Take me to thee, and thee to mee:
No, no, no, no, my Deare, let bee.

Astrophel and Stella

Night hath closde all in her cloke,
Twinkling starres loue–thoughts prouoke,
Danger hence, good care doth keepe,
Iealouzie hemselfe doth sleepe;
Take me to thee, and thee to mee:
No, no, no, no, my Deare, let bee.

Better place no wit can finde,
Cupids knot to loose or binde;
These sweet flowers our fine bed too,
Vs in their best language woo:
Take me to thee, and thee to mee:
No, no, no, no, my Deare, let bee.

This small light the moone bestowes
Serues thy beames but to disclose;
So to raise my hap more hie,
Feare not else, none vs can spie;
Take me to thee, and thee to mee:
No, no, no, no, my Deare, let bee.

That you heard was but a mouse,
Dumbe Sleepe holdeth all the house:
Yet asleepe, me thinkes they say,
Yong fooles take time while you may;
Take me to thee, and thee to mee:
No, no, no, no, my Deare, let bee.

Niggard time threates, if we misse
This large offer of our blisse,
Long stay, ere he graunt the same:
Sweet, then, while ech thing doth frame,
Take me to thee, and thee to mee:
No, no, no, no, my Deare, let bee.

Astrophel and Stella

Your faire Mother is abed,
Candles out and curtaines spred;
She thinkes you do letters write;
Write, but first let me endite;
Take me to thee, and thee to mee:
No, no, no, no, my Deare, let bee.

Sweete, alas, why striue you thus?
Concord better fitteth vs;
Leaue to Mars the force of hands,
Your power in your beautie stands;
Take me to thee, and thee to mee:
No, no, no, no, my Deare, let bee.

Wo to mee, and do you sweare
Me to hate, but I forbeare?
Cursed be my destines all,
That brought me so high to fall;
Soone with my death I will please thee:
No, no, no, no, my Deare, let bee.

Fift Song.

While fauour fed my hope, delight with hope was brought,
Thought waited on delight, and speech did follow thought;
Then grew my tongue and pen records vnto thy glory,
I thought all words were lost that were not spent of thee,
I thought each place was darke but where thy lights would be,
And all eares worse than deaf that heard not out thy storie.

I said thou wert most faire, and so indeed thou art;
I said thou wert most sweet, sweet poison to my heart;

Astrophel and Stella

I said my soule was thine, O that I then had lyed;
I said thine eyes were starres, thy breast the milken way,
Thy fingers Cupids shafts, thy voyce the angels lay:
And all I said so well, as no man it denied.

But now that hope is lost, vnkindnesse kils delight;
Yet thought and speech do liue, though metamorphos'd quite,
For rage now rules the raines which guided were by pleasure;
I thinke now of thy faults, who late thought of thy praise,
That speech falles now to blame, which did thy honour raise,
The same key open can, which can lock vp a treasure.

Then thou, whom partiall heauens conspird in one to frame
The proofe of Beauties worth, th'inheritrix of fame,
The mansion seat of blisse, and iust excuse of louers;
See now those feathers pluckt, wherewith thou flew'st most high:
See what cloudes of reproach shall dark thy honours skie:
Whose owne fault cast him downe hardly high state recouers.

And, O my muse, though oft you luld her in your lap,
And then a heau'nly Child, gaue her Ambrosian pap,
And to that braine of hers your kindest gifts infused;
Since she, disdaining me, doth you in me disdaine,
Suffer not her to laugh, while both we suffer paine.
Princes in subiects wrong must deeme themselues abused.

Your client, poore my selfe, shall Stella handle so!
Reuenge! revenge! my Muse! defiance trumpet blow;
Threaten what may be done, yet do more then you threaten;
Ah, my sute granted is, I feele my breast doth swell;
No, child, a lesson new you shall begin to spell,
Sweet babes must babies haue, but shrewd gyrles must be beaten.

Thinke now no more to heare of warme fine–odour'd snow,
Nor blushing Lillies, nor pearles Ruby–hidden row,
Nor of that golden sea, whose waues in curles are broken,

Astrophel and Stella

But of thy soule, so fraught with such vngratefulnesse,
As where thou soone might'st helpe, most faith dost most oppresse;
Vngratefull, who is cald, the worst of euils is spoken,

Yet worse then worst, I say thou art a Theefe, A theefe!
Now God forbid! a theefe! and of wurst theeues the cheefe:
Theeues steal for need, and steale but goods which paine recouers,
But thou, rich in all ioyes, dost rob my ioyes from me,
Which cannot be restord by time or industrie:
Of foes the spoyle is euill, far worse of constant louers.

Yet—gentle English theeues do rob, but will not slay,
Thou English murdring theefe, wilt haue harts for thy prey:
The name of murdrer now on thy faire forehead sitteth,
And euen while I do speake, my death wounds bleeding be,
Which, I protest, proceed from only cruell thee:
Who may, and will not saue, murder in truth committeth.

But murder, priuate fault, seemes but a toy to thee:
I lay then to thy charge vniustest tyrannie,
If rule by force, without all claim, a Tyran showeth;
For thou dost lord my heart, who am not borne thy slaue,
And, which is worse, makes me, most guiltlesse, torments haue:
A rightfull prince by vnright deeds a Tyran groweth.

Lo, you grow proud with this, for Tyrans make folke bow:
Of foule rebellion then I do appeach thee now,
Rebell by Natures law, rebell by law of Reason:
Thou, sweetest subiect wert, borne in the realme of Loue,
And yet against thy prince thy force dost daily proue:
No vertue merits praise, once toucht with blot of Treason.

But valiant Rebels oft in fooles mouths purchase fame:
I now then staine thy white with vagabonding shame,
Both rebell to the sonne and vagrant from the mother;
For wearing Venus badge in euery part of thee,

Astrophel and Stella

Vnto Dianaes traine thou, runnaway, didst flie:
Who faileth one is false, though trusty to another.

What, is not this enough! nay, farre worse commeth here;
A witch, I say, thou art, though thou so faire appeare;
For, I protest, my sight neuer thy face enioyeth,
But I in me am chang'd, I am aliue and dead,
My feete are turn'd to rootes, my hart becommeth lead:
No witchcraft is so euill as which mans mind destroyeth.

Yet witches may repent; thou art farre worse then they:
Alas that I am forst such euill of thee to say:
I say thou art a diuell, though cloth'd in angels shining;
For thy face tempts my soule to leaue the heauens for thee,
And thy words of refuse do powre euen hell on mee:
Who tempt, and tempting plague, are diuels in true defining.

You, then, vngrateful theefe, you murdring Tyran, you,
You rebell runaway, to lord and lady vntrue,
You witch, you Diuell (alas) you still of me beloued,
You see what I can say; mend yet your froward mind,
And such skill in my Muse, you, reconcil'd, shall find,
That all these cruell words your praises shalbe proued.

Sixt Song.

O you that heare this voice,
O you that see this face,
Say whether of the choice
Deserues the former place:
Feare not to iudge this bate,
For it is void of hate.

Astrophel and Stella

This side doth Beauty take.
For that doth Musike speake;
Fit Oratours to make
The strongest iudgements weake:
The barre to plead their right
Is only true delight.

Thus doth the voice and face,
These gentle Lawiers, wage,
Like louing brothers case,
For fathers heritage;
That each, while each contends,
It selfe to other lends.

For Beautie beautifies
With heau'nly hew and grace
The heau'nly harmonies;
And in this faultlesse face
The perfect beauties be
A perfect harmony.

Musick more loftly swels
In speeches nobly plac'd;
Beauty as farre excels,
In action aptly grac'd:
A friend each party draws
To countenance his cause.

Loue more affected seemes
To Beauties louely light;
And Wonder more esteemes
Of Musickes wondrous might;
But both to both so bent,
As both in both are spent.

Musicke doth witnesse call
The eare his truth to trie;
Beauty brings to the hall
Eye—iudgement of the eye:
Both in their obiects such,
As no exceptions tutch.

The common sense, which might
Be arbiter of this,
To be, forsooth, vpright,
To both sides partiall is;
He layes on this chiefe praise,
Chiefe praise on that he laies.

Then reason, princesse hy,
Whose throne is in the minde,
Which Musicke can in sky
And hidden beauties finde,
Say whether thou wilt crowne
With limitlesse renowne?

Seuenth Song.

Whose senses in so euill consort their stepdame Nature laies,
That rauishing delight in them most sweete tunes do not raise;
Or if they do delight therein, yet are so closde with wit,
As with ententious lips to set a title vaine on it;
O let them heare these sacred tunes, and learne in Wonders scholes,
To be, in things past bounds of wit, fooles: if they be not fooles.

Who haue so leaden eyes, as not to see sweet Beauties show,
Or, seeing, haue so wooden wits, as not that worth to know,

Or, knowing, haue so muddy minds, as not to be in loue,
Or, louing, haue so frothy thoughts, as eas'ly thence to moue;
O let them see these heau'nly beames, and in faire letters reede
A lesson fit, both sight and skill, loue and firme loue to breede.

Heare then, but then with wonder heare, see, but adoring, see,
No mortall gifts, no earthly fruites, now here descended be:
See, doo you see this face? a face, nay, image of the skies,
Of which the two life–giuing lights are figur'd in her eyes:
Heare you this soule–inuading voice, and count it but a voice?
The very essence of their tunes, when angels do reioyce.

Eight Song.

In a groue most rich of shade,
Where birds wanton musicke made,
Maie, then yong, his pide weedes showing,
New–perfum'd with flowers fresh growing:

Astrophel with Stella sweet
Did for mutual comfort meete,
Both within themselues oppressed,
But each in the other blessed.

Him great harmes had taught much care,
Her faire necke a foule yoke bare;
But her sight his cares did banish,
In his sight her yoke did vanish:

Wept they had, alas, the while,
But now teares themselues did smile,
While their eyes, by Loue directed,

Astrophel and Stella

Enterchangeably reflected.

Sigh they did; but now betwixt
Sighes of woe were glad sighes mixt;
With arms crost, yet testifying
restlesse rest, and liuing dying.

Their eares hungrie of each word
Which the deare tongue would afford;
But their tongues restrain'd from walking,
Till their harts had ended talking.

But when their tongues could not speake,
Loue it selfe did silence breake;
Loue did set his lips asunder,
Thus to speake in loue and wonder.

Stella, Soueraigne of my ioy,
Faire triumpher of annoy;
Stella, Starre of heauenly fier,
Stella, loadstar of desier;

Stella, in whose shining eyes
Are the lights of Cupids skies,
Whose beames, where they once are darted,
Loue therewith is streight imparted;

Stella, whose voice when it speakes
Senses all asunder breakes;
Stella, whose voice, when it singeth,
Angels to acquaintance bringeth;

Stella, in whose body is
Writ each caracter of blisse;
Whose face all, all beauty passeth,
Saue thy mind, which it surpasseth.

Astrophel and Stella

Graunt, O graunt; but speach, alas,
Failes me, fearing on to passe:
Graunt, O me: what am I saying?
But no fault there is in praying.

Graunt (O Deere) on knees I pray,
(Knees on ground he then did stay)
That, not I, but since I loue you,
Time and place for me may moue you.

Neuer season was more fit;
Never roome more apt for it;
Smiling ayre allowes my reason;
These birds sing, Now vse the season.

This small wind, which so sweete is,
See how it the leaues doth kisse;
Each tree in his best attiring,
Sense of Loue to Loue inspiring.

Loue makes earth the water drink,
Loue to earth makes water sinke;
And, if dumbe things be so witty,
Shall a heauenly Grace want pitty?

There his hands, in their speech, faine
Would haue made tongues language plaine;
But her hands, his hands repelling,
Gaue repulse all grace expelling.

Then she spake; her speech was such,
So not eares, but hart did tuch:
While such—wise she loue denied,
And yet loue she signified.

Astrophel and Stella

Astrophel, sayd she, my loue,
Cease, in these effects, to proue;
Now be still, yet still beleeue me,
Thy griefe more then death would grieue me.

If that any thought in me
Can tast comfort but of thee,
Let me, fed with hellish anguish,
Ioylesse, hopelesse, endlesse languish.

If those eyes you praised be
Halfe so deare as you to me,
Let me home returne, starke blinded
Of those eyes, and blinder minded;

If to secret of my hart,
I do any wish impart,
Where thou art not formost placed,
Be both wish and I defaced.

If more may be sayd, I say,
All my blisse in thee I lay;
If thou loue, my loue, content thee,
For all loue, all faith is meant thee.

Trust me, while I thee deny,
In my selfe the smart I try;
Tyran Honour doth thus vse thee,
Stellas selfe might not refuse thee.

Therefore, deare, this no more moue,
Least, though I leaue not thy loue,
Which too deep in me is framed,
I should blush when thou art named.

Therewithall away she went,

Leauing him to passion rent,
With what she had done and spoken,
That therewith my song is broken.

Ninth Song.

Go, my Flocke, go, get you hence,
Seeke a better place of feeding,
Where you may haue some defence
Fro the stormes in my breast breeding,
And showers from mine eyes proceeding.

Leaue a wretch, in whom all wo
Can abide to keepe no measure;
Merry Flocke, such one forego,
Vnto whom mirth is displeasure,
Onely rich in mischiefs treasure.

Yet, alas, before you go,
Heare your wofull Maisters story,
Which to stones I els would show:
Sorrow only then hath glory
When 'tis excellently sorry.

Stella, fiercest shepherdesse,
Fiercest, but yet fairest euer;
Stella, whom, O heauens still blesse,
Though against me she perseuer,
Though I blisse enherit neuer:

Stella hath refused me!
Stella, who more loue hath proued,

Astrophel and Stella

In this caitife heart to be,
Then can in good eawes be moued
Toward Lambkins best beloued.

Stella hath refused me!
Astrophell, that so well served
In this pleasant Spring must see,
While in pride flowers be preserued,
Himselfe onely Winter–sterued.

Why (alas) doth she then sweare
That she loueth me so dearely,
Seeing me so long to beare
Coles of loue that burne so cleerly,
And yet leaue me helplesse meerely?

Is that loue? forsooth, I trow,
If I saw my good dog grieued,
And a helpe for him did know,
My loue should not be beleeued,
But he were by me releeued.

No, she hates me, well–away,
Faining loue, somewhat to please me:
For she knows, if she display
All her hate, death soone would seaze me,
And of hideous torments ease me.

Then adieu, deare Flocke, adieu;
But, alas, if in your straying
Heauenly Stella meete with you,
Tell her, in your pitious blaying,
Her poore Slaues vniust decaying.

Astrophel and Stella

Tenth Song.

O deare Life, when shall it bee
That mine eyes thine eyes shall see,
And in them thy mind discouer
Whether absence haue had force
thy remembrance to diuorce
From the image of thy louer?

Or if I my self find not,
After parting aught forgot,
Nor debar'd from Beauties treasure,
Let not tongue aspire to tell
In what high ioyes I shall dwell;
Only thought aymes at the pleasure.

Thought, therefore, I will send thee
To take vp the place for me:
Long I will not after tary,
There vnseene, thou mayst be bold,
Those faire wonders to behold,
Which in them my hopes do cary.

Thought, see thou no place forbeare,
Enter brauely euerywhere,
Seize on all to her belonging;
But if thou wouldst garded be,
Fearing her beames, take with thee
Strength of liking, rage of longing.

Thinke of that most gratefull time
When my leaping heart will climb,
In thy lips to haue his biding,
There those roses for to kisse,
Which do breathe a sugred blisse,

Opening rubies, pearles diuiding.

Thinke of my most princely pow'r,
Which I blessed shall deuow'r
With my greedy licorous sences,
Beauty, musicke, sweetnesse, loue,
While she doth against me proue
Her strong darts but weake defences.

Thinke, thinke of those dalyings,
When with doue–like murmurings,
With glad moning, passed anguish,
We change eyes, and hart for hart,
Each to other do depart,
Ioying till ioy makes vs languish.

O my Thoughts, my Thoughts surcease,
Thy delights my woes increse,
My life melts with too much thinking;
Thinke no more, but die in me,
Till thou shalt reuiued be,
At her lips my Nectar drinking.

Eleuenth Song.

Who is it that this darke night
Vnderneath my window playneth?
It is one who from thy sight
Being, ah exil'd, disdayneth
Euery other vulgar light.

Why, alas, and are you he?

Astrophel and Stella

Be not yet those fancies changed?
Deare, when you find change in me,
Though from me you be estranged,
Let my chaunge to ruin be.

Well, in absence this will dy;
Leaue to see, and leaue to wonder.
Absence sure will helpe, if I
Can learne how my selfe to sunder
From what in my hart doth ly.

But time will these thoughts remoue;
Time doth work what no man knoweth.
Time doth as the subiect proue;
With time still the affection groweth
In the faithful turtle–doue.

What if we new beauties see,
Will they not stir new affection?
I will thinke they pictures be,
(Image–like, of saints perfection)
Poorely counterfeting thee.

But your reasons purest light
Bids you leaue such minds to nourish.
Deere, do reason no such spite;
Neuer doth thy beauty florish
More then in my reasons sight.

But the wrongs Loue beares will make
Loue at length leaue vndertaking.
No, the more fooles it doth shake,
In a ground of so firme making
Deeper still they driue the stake.

Peace, I thinke that some giue eare;

Astrophel and Stella

Come no more, least I get anger.
Blisse, I will my blisse forbeare;
Fearing, sweete, you to endanger;
But my soule shall harbour there.

Well, be gone; be gone, I say,
Lest that Argus eyes perceiue you.
O vniust is Fortunes sway,
Which can make me thus to leaue you,
And from lowts to run away.

—

CPSIA information can be obtained
at www.ICGtesting.com
Printed in the USA
LVHW062205120319
610449LV00017B/170/P